Edinburgh Castle

Text by Richard Fawcett,
Iain MacIvor and Bent Petersen
Edited by Nicholas Reynolds

Designed by
HMSO Graphic Design   Edinburgh

Principal photography by
The Graham Falconer Visual Arts Group
Edinburgh (photographers Graham
Falconer and Sean Hudson)

ISBN 0 11 491676 4

Edinburgh
Her Majesty's Stationery Office

*Grateful thanks for permission to
reproduce photographs to*

The Scottish Tourist Board
The Royal Commission on the Ancient
and Historical Monuments of Scotland
The National Library of Scotland
Edinburgh City Library
The Scottish National Portrait Gallery
The Scottish United Services Museum
The Scottish National War Memorial
Craig Lindsay
Brian Swinburne

Introduction

Edinburgh Castle's association with the history of the Scottish nation is a long one, and for many visitors the Castle is seen as the most tangible embodiment of that history. But its own architectural history as a group of buildings erected for specific, but changing needs is also highly fascinating, and the visitor who attempts to come to some understanding of this will find the effort rewarding.

The starting point of any study of the Castle must be the rock on which it stands: a magnificent and naturally strong site formed by the core of an extinct volcano. The action of glaciers in the Ice Ages left near-vertical faces on the north and south sides, with a more gradual slope on the west, and a gently descending ridge on the east. It is tempting to suggest that such a site must have been rendered defensible since prehistoric times, but there is no physical evidence to support this idea, and the earliest reference we have to its occupation is in the 6th century. Even then our knowledge of its use is very shadowy, and it is not until the 11th century that we begin to be able to see it as a Castle.

It is important to remember that Edinburgh was not the 'capital' of Scotland in any modern sense until the very end of the Middle Ages – before that time the capital was

wherever the king and his court happened to be, and Edinburgh was only one of several important centres. But the Castle was certainly a favourite residence of the Scottish kings from at least the 11th century, and it was here that St Margaret died, shortly after hearing of the death of her husband, King Malcolm III, and her eldest son, in 1093. The oldest surviving building in the Castle, the Chapel, is dedicated to her memory, although it was probably not built until after her youngest son, David I, came to the throne in 1124.

Apart from the Chapel we know virtually nothing of the earliest buildings of the Castle. Between 1174 and 1186 it was held by an English garrison, following the capture of King William the Lion at Alnwick, and it was again taken by the English in 1296, although it was to change hands on several occasions in the course of Scotland's struggle for independence of English domination. The Castle's defences were demolished by the Scots themselves in 1313, because they did not wish it to be held against them by the English, and it was only when King David II started major rebuilding after his return from English captivity in 1356 that the Castle walls began to assume their present form. Throughout the Middle Ages the Castle was largely confined to the highest point of the rock summit, and David concentrated on building a strong defensive line across the main approach to the Castle from the east, with a great tower (later known as David's Tower) for his residence towards the south end. This work was continued by his successor, Robert II, who added a gate-tower at the north end of the cross-wall, with a residence for his Constable on its upper floors.

Successive kings progressively augmented the royal accommodation within the Castle, and it is likely that a chamber which James I is known to have built for himself to the south of David's Tower in the 1430s was on the site of the later Palace block. However, most of the structures referred to in the surviving building records have left little immediately apparent trace in the Castle, and it is only from the reigns of James IV and his successors that substantial remains of the buildings within the Castle walls begin to survive in recognisable form. In the first years of the 16th century James IV completed a fine Great Hall, which had to be built out on a massive sub-structure along the south side of the Castle, and it was probably also he who began to give the southern part of the Palace-building the form it now has.

By this date Edinburgh's role as the most important Castle of the kingdom, and to an increasing extent as the seat of government was becoming more apparent: it had been the principal store and manufactury of royal artillery for some time, and in the 1540s a repository was built here for the state records. It is perhaps fortunate for our understanding of the Castle that in 1544 Edinburgh was attacked by an English force and a record drawing was made of this event by an English agent, which includes the first accurate representation of the Castle. It shows David's Tower at one end of the wall which crossed the east side of the Castle rock, with a circular tower at the other end which appears to form part of the Constable's Tower gatehouse; sheltering

Edinburgh Castle at the time of the siege by the Earl of Hertford's army, 1544.

'Edinburgum Scotiae Metropolis' c 1582. Braun and Hogenburg, Amsterdam.

3

Sir William Kirkcaldy of
Grange by Clouet.

Edinburgh Castle in 1647,
after Gordon of Rothiemay.

Edinburgh Castle *c* 1780 by
Alexander Nasmyth.

behind the walls are a number of smaller buildings. For the first time we have a relatively clear picture of how the Castle must have looked.

Although the Castle had not been seriously threatened in this attack it was decided to increase the defences immediately afterwards, and an Italian engineer was commissioned to build an artillery bastion in front of the cross-wall. It is probably true to say that the Castle's military and political significance was by now beginning to outweigh its function as a royal residence, except at times of emergency, and more comfortably spacious accommodation for the royal household was found elsewhere, as in the Abbey of Holyrood. Mary Queen of Scots chose to give birth to her son in the Castle in 1566, probably more because of its symbolic importance than because of the convenience of its royal apartment.

In the second half of the 16th century Scotland was torn by great internal conflicts, and the Castle was at the heart of much of these. In 1573 the walls were blasted to pieces when Kirkcaldy of Grange attempt to hold it for Queen Mary, and in the course of the ensuing fifteen years the defences on the east side of the Castle rock were transformed. The ruins of David's Tower were completely enveloped by a massive curved wall topped by an artillery platform, known as the Half Moon Battery, and a greatly strengthened cross-wall capped by the Forewall Battery was erected across the rock. A new gatehouse, now known as the Portcullis Gate, was built to replace the gatehouse in the old Constable's tower. Further major works were undertaken between 1615 and 1617 in anticipation of James VI's first homecoming after he had been crowned as James I of England in 1603. But these works were largely domestic, and involved the extension of the Palace block to provide suitable accommodation for the King.

An engraving of 1647 shows the Castle much as it must have looked at that time. Although the whole of the plateau on top of the rock is depicted as being surrounded by wall, the Castle itself is still almost entirely confined to the highest part of the rock, with the Palace and Hall around two sides of a courtyard, and a munition house (which had originally been built as a church) on the third side. The small chapel of St Margaret, by this time extended and in use as a powder magazine, stands some distance to the north, and the Half Moon Battery, bristling with guns, overlooks the approaches from the town. In front of the Castle is the patched-up bastion which had been built in the 1540s.

After this date the Castle's residual royal role almost entirely disappeared, although in 1672 part of the Palace range was fitted up as an official residence for the Duke of Lauderdale, as Commissioner to the Scottish parliament. But this was exceptional. Passing mention has already been made of the secularisation of the Castle's two places of worship, and in the 1650s Cromwell's force of occupation had begun to convert the royal buildings to military uses by sub-dividing the Great Hall to form barracks. From now on the Castle's prime function was that of a fortress and barrack, and it was this that dictated what building operations took place. The ditch across the entrance front was started in the 1650s, and in the 1670s major works of improvement were made to the defences. Further schemes for vast outer defences were started in 1708, but were abandoned unfinished shortly afterwards, although at the same time a new officers' barrack block was built on the west side of the Castle's main square. Repairs and reconstruction of the walls were again undertaken in the 1720s and 1740s, and in 1742 an elegant house was built for the Governor to the north-west of the main complex of buildings.

In the course of these years the Castle had suffered several assaults, some of which necessitated the considerable works of reparation and augmentation which have already been mentioned. In 1640 General Leslie had besieged and taken the Castle for the Covenanters, and in 1650 it was taken for Cromwell. The Duke of Gordon unsuccessfully attempted to defend the Castle for James VII against the forces of William and Mary in 1689, and in 1715 the Jacobites made an attempt to take the Castle for the Old Pretender. The last action which the Castle saw was in the '45, when the Young Pretender's forces made another half-hearted effort to take the Castle.

By the second half of the 18th century the Castle's defences had reached the form which we now see, and from this date onwards building activity was mainly concentrated on the structures within the Castle walls. Between 1748 and 1754 a new powder-magazine, flanked by ordnance-stores, was built at the west end of the rock, and in 1796 the vast New Barracks were built towards the south of the rock to accommodate the soldiers fighting in the wars with France. But by the early 19th century this strictly utilitarian attitude to the Castle was beginning to be modified by a new awareness of its historical importance – and

Prince Charles Edward Stuart by Antonio David.

View of the Castle in 1719.

perhaps also its Romantic associations. Although much building and rebuilding was still taking place, efforts were now made to ensure that any new work could be considered appropriate for its setting. It is interesting to note that Sir Walter Scott was closely involved in this change of attitudes.

In 1846 St Margaret's Chapel was rediscovered amongst the clutter of later buildings, and restored to what was thought to be its 12th century form; and in 1858 work started on the reconstruction of some of the western walls to a more picturesque profile, but was abandoned incomplete because of public protest. Several schemes were put forward for 'improvements' on a gargantuan scale, including one proposal which would have

Proposed restorations and additions, 1859.

The Old Ordnance Stores around 1870.

Edinburgh Castle *c* 1856 by Thomas Keith.

involved almost total rebuilding of the Castle, and for which a series of superb drawings survives.

19th century photographs certainly show that many of the lesser buildings which stood at that time were somewhat bland, and it is easy to understand the attitudes of romantically inclined architects who wished to make the Castle worthy of its history – although we should probably be grateful that many of these schemes went no further than the drawing board. Nevertheless, a photograph of the old ordnance stores, for example, shows how characterless the external face presented by some of the more mundane buildings was, and the extensive remodelling of this group of buildings in 1896 to form a new hospital should perhaps not be regretted. Probably the most significant works of restoration were those on the Great Hall and Portcullis gate in the 1880s, whilst at the same time a new entrance-front was built on the east side of the Castle, overlooking the Esplanade. The last major operation was the construction of the Scottish National War Memorial in the 1920s; the Castle has seen very few structural changes since then.

The end-result of this long history is a fascinating complex of structures which, as a whole, represent no one period of the Castle's story, but which individually show how each succeeding generation has modified what it inherited to its own particular requirements. The attempt to understand how each of these buildings assumed its present form, and how this was dictated by its function and its relationship with the other buildings, requires a considerable effort, but one which is well-worth making by those who wish to get the most from their visit to the Castle.

Tour

1 THE ESPLANADE

The open area in front of the Castle, known as the Esplanade, is essentially the ridge which resulted from the action of glaciers on the extinct volcano forming the Castle Rock. But in its present form it owes as much to human as to natural action. The ridge was levelled and widened to form a parade-ground in the mid-18th century, using the waste from the site of the Exchange (now the City Chambers) on the north side of High Street for this purpose. The ornamental walls which run along each side were added between 1816 and 1820. It now forms a spacious prelude to the Castle, and commands splendid views over Edinburgh and the surrounding countryside.

2 THE GATEHOUSE

Because this was always the most vulnerable side of the Castle, and also its natural entrance point, the main defences have always been concentrated on this side, although they have taken a number of different forms in the course of the Castle's history. The existing Gatehouse was built in 1887, by which time it was not considered necessary to make the Castle seriously defensible, and so its design was simply an attempt to create an entrance worthy of the Castle it represented, without any regard to military or historical logic. It was further embellished when the statues of Robert the Bruce and William Wallace were added on either side of the entrance in 1929. However, although the design of the Gatehouse owes nothing to previous buildings on the site, its plan, at least, was conditioned by the existing defences, because it was decided to retain the ditch which cuts off the approach to the Castle Rock from the esplanade. This ditch had been started by Cromwell's army in the 1650s, although it was not to be finished until almost a hundred years later. To allow adequate coverage of the ditch from the ramparts behind, it was cut in a hollow three-sided shape, and this shape was repeated in the Gatehouse of 1887. It is interesting to note that the retractable bridge which was provided for the Gatehouse was the last drawbridge to be built in Scotland.

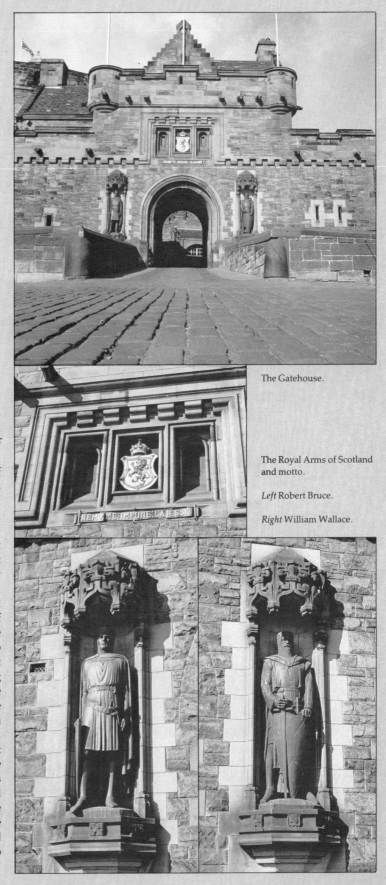

The Gatehouse.

The Royal Arms of Scotland and motto.

Left Robert Bruce.

Right William Wallace.

9

The Half Moon Battery from below.

Plaque in memory of Kirkcaldy of Grange on lower wall of Forewall Battery.

IN MEMORY OF SIR WILLIAM KIRKCALDY
GRANGE JUSTLY REPUTED TO BE ONE OF THE BEST
SOLDIERS AND MOST ACCOMPLISHED CAVALIERS
OF HIS TIME HE HELD THIS CASTLE FOR QUEEN
MARY FROM MAY 1568 TO MAY 1573 AND AFTER
ITS HONOURABLE SURRENDER SUFFERED DEATH
FOR DEVOTION TO HER CAUSE ON 3RD AUGUST 1573

3 THE HALF MOON BATTERY

Until the 17th century the principal defensive line of the Castle was set back behind the present outer defences, and the massive walls which confront the visitor once he is through the Gatehouse are approximately on the line of the wall which was built across the east side of the rock in the 14th century. However all of what is now seen dates from the 16th century or later. On the left side is the great curved wall of the Half Moon Battery which was built in the 1570s to provide a platform for artillery which could overlook the approaches to the Castle on this side. Incapsulated within the walls of the battery are the shattered remains of a tower-house built for David II in 1368, which was knocked down in the course of the siege in 1573.

4 THE FOREWALL BATTERY

To the right of the Half Moon Battery is the straight wall of the Forewall Battery. As it now stands it is mainly of the same date as the Half Moon Battery, although it incorporates part of a wall built in the 1540s. Below the junction of the two batteries the access road passes through the Inner Barrier, which was built in the 18th century, and originally provided a more formidable obstacle than now, because it had a ditch in front of it.

5 THE PORTCULLIS GATE

At the head of the approach road is the principal gateway of the Castle as reconstructed in the 1570s (the gate into the mediaeval castle, known as the Constable's tower, was probably also somewhere in this area, although its precise site is no longer known). The lower storeys of the gate are enlivened with Renaissance decoration, including the arms of the Earl of Morton, who was Regent of Scotland at the time it was built. The upper stages of the gate date from 1886, and replace a simple 18th century roof.

Opposite The Portcullis Gate.

6 THE ARGYLE BATTERY

The area of the Castle immediately inside the Portcullis Gate gives little impression of how the rock top must have looked throughout the Middle Ages. The existing wide roads and flat areas are entirely artificial, and replace what must have been a rather rugged expanse until the 17th century. Before that date the main part of the Castle was up on the highest point of the rock, to left of the Portcullis Gate, and was approached by the steep staircase within the gate which is still there, although there was certainly also an outer curtain wall of some form around the whole of the rock top. The battery to the right of the gate, known as the Argyle or Six Gun Battery was built in the 1730s for Major General Wade, who is probably best known in Scotland as the designer of a network of military roads and bridges.

The Argyle Battery and details including the One O'clock Gun, Mills Mount Battery and the Low Defence.

7 MILL'S MOUNT BATTERY

Beyond the Argyle Battery is Mill's Mount Battery, which similarly looks out to the north, and gives splendid views of Princes Street Gardens and the 18th century New Town of Edinburgh. It now requires an effort of imagination to realise that, when these batteries were built, Edinburgh was mainly confined to the Old Town, stretching eastwards to Holyrood, and that the area of the New Town was still open fields. It is from this battery that the one o'clock gun is fired every day.

8 THE LOW DEFENCE

At a lower level than these batteries are artillery outworks known as the Low Defence. They may have been first built in the 1540s to provide flanking support for an artillery spur built on the east side of the Castle, although in their present form they are of 17th and 18th century date. At a later date they appear to have served a second purpose as a garden for the Governor, although it is difficult to imagine what plants may have been grown here.

9 CART-SHED

To the left of Mill's Mount Battery is a mid-18th century Cart-Shed, covered by a series of double-pitched roofs. It has been much altered in more than two centuries of existence, and it has also served as a barrack and an ammunition store; it is now used as a tea-room.

10 THE GOVERNOR'S HOUSE

The Governor's House is a pleasingly restrained classical building erected in 1742; its crow-stepped gables were perhaps a little old-fashioned for so late a date. On each side of it are low wings which were built to house the Master Gunner and Store-keeper. The house is now used as the Officers' Mess of the Castle garrison, although the wing on the right side is still the official residence of the Governor. Rising behind this building is the overwhelming mass of the New Barracks, built in the 1790s, which dwarfs all else in the Castle.

11 THE HOSPITAL

On a lower level to the west of the Cart-Shed and Governor's House, and reached by way of a road between them, is the hospital. This group of buildings has a complicated history. A powder magazine built here in 1679 was replaced by a new building in 1748, which was itself augmented in 1753 by flanking Ordnance Storehouses to form an enclosed courtyard. 19th century photographs show that the resulting structures presented a rather plain front to the outside world, and in the 1890s, at the height of the period of 'improvements' to the Castle, it was decided to remodel them to form a hospital. The powder magazine was removed altogether, whilst the north block was heightened and completely reconstructed in an early 17th century style. The south block was less thoroughly altered, and its lower storey towards the courtyard still has, in modified form, the arcade with which it was first built.

The action of glaciers moving from west to east left the west side of the Castle rock less steep than the north and south faces. On the west side the rock descends to the crags at its base in a series of terraces, or steps, and it was in response to the these that the defences were built at two different levels from at least 17th century onwards. At the upper level is a terrace, constructed in its present form in 1858, which runs along the north and west sides of the Hospital; adverse public reactions prevented the addition of a large projecting bastion which was planned at that time to increase the picturesque appearance of the upper wall. 17th and 18th century plans of the Castle show that the earlier wall at this point had been severely functional, and ran directly beneath the walls of what is now the hospital.

The lower walls of the Western Defences run above the crags at the base of the rock's west side, and their irregular plan is dictated by the natural formation of the site. In their present form they date mainly from the 1730s, although the first attempt to create a walkway behind walls at the lower level was made in the reign of Charles II. There are sentry boxes at two of the changes in angle of the wall: the northern one is known as the Queen's Post, whilst the southern one is close to the site of a small postern gate of the Castle. A stair within a turret at the southern junction of the two levels of the western defences was the principal means of access between the two.

Rear of New Barracks from the Old Back Parade.

Gordon Highlanders at the Castle in Victorian times, D O Hill.

Stairs up to Dury's Battery.

Bottom Dury's Battery.

13 BUTTS BATTERY

In their present form the defences on the south side of the Castle date from the years between 1708 and 1713. In 1708 a French squadron had sailed into the Firth of Forth in support of an attempt to win the throne for the son of James VII (the Old Pretender) and, although that attempt was unsuccessful, it led to real fears of insurrection north of the Border. As a consequence the principle Scottish castles were put into a state of preparedness by the military engineer for Scotland, Theodore Dury. Amongst his various proposals for Edinburgh was a scheme for a vast outwork to the east of the Castle, but work on this was abandoned soon after it was started, and Dury had to content himself with improvements to the accommodation within the Castle, and to the perimeter defences, of which Butts Battery was a part. The battery takes its name from the fact that the bow butts, where the archers practised firing at targets, used to be in this area.

14 OLD BACK PARADE

The area known as the Old Back Parade is now completely overshadowed by the enormous new barracks, which were built in the 1790s. Because of the slope of the rock-top on the south, it was necessary to build a sub-structure for the building on this side, and the large arches, which now appear to be simply a decorative device, were open to the elements, until they were infilled in the 19th century. It is noticeable that the architecture of the barracks is very austere on this side, and that there are few embellishments such as those which relieve its ponderous mass on the north side. As a general rule it appears to be true that the designers of 18th century buildings within the Castle made little attempt to present anything but an austere face to the outside world, and it was as a reaction to this that attempts were made to 'improve' the Castle in the following century.

15 DURY'S BATTERY

The name of Theodore Dury, who rebuilt the Castle's southern walls in the early years of the 18th century, is commemorated in the name of this Battery. Because of the con-figurations of the rock it is at a considerably higher level than Butts Battery and the Old Back Parade, and the two levels are connected by a long flght of steps.

16 THE MILITARY PRISON

Behind Dury's Battery is the small Military Prison, which was built in about 1842. It is an interesting building for two reasons: in the first place because it dates from a period when much thought was being given to the purpose and design of prisons, and in the second place because its final design was part of the effort to give the buildings within the Castle a form which could be considered appropriate for their historic setting. The prison was designed to accommodate offenders from all Scottish garrisons, not just Edinburgh Castle, and its form was dictated by the need to provide solitary confinement for all its inmates. Two levels of cells surround a central space, with cast iron galleries running around the upper level. The cells themselves, whilst being rather less than homely, are quite spacious, and were capable of being centrally heated. Externally an architectural interest was given to the building by variety of forms and the way in which the parts were grouped in relation to each other. The prison was last used in 1923.

17 THE FRENCH PRISONS

When the Great Hall was built on the south side of the Castle Rock at the turn of the 15th and 16th centuries, it was necessary to erect a series of great vaulted substructures above the sloping rock-face to create a level surface for the hall floor at the height of the Castle's main square. These vaults, however, were not confined simply to the area of the hall, but were extended to the west, under the area which is now occupied by the Scottish United Services Museum. Although the vaults were only a means to the end of obtaining a good level for the upper building, they have been put to a number of uses throughout their history, including an arsenal, a barrack, a bakehouse and stores. But the use for which they are best remembered is that of accommodation for foreign prisoners-of-war, and particularly for the soldiers captured in the wars with France in the second half of the 18th and the early 19th centuries. Some of the graffiti scrawled by the prisoners are still to be seen, particularly in the stonework of the main entrance door, which opens to one side of Dury's Battery. An interesting side-light on the life of the prisoners is to be seen in a number of surviving pieces of handicraft which they sold to obtain money for themselves, including the particularly fine ship-model which is now displayed in the Scottish United Services Museum.

One of the vaults now contains the magnificent siege-gun, of a type known as a *bombard*, which goes by the name of Mons Meg. This gun was made in the 1440s for the Duke of Burgundy, probably at Mons in modern Belgium, and was sent to his nephew-by-marriage, James II, in 1457. It had a long and eventful career in Scottish service until it burst when firing a salute in 1681, and was then abandoned. Later, it was for many years displayed in the Tower of London, until it was returned to Edinburgh in 1829, where it was displayed in the open, close to St Margaret's Chapel. It was found that the weather was having ill effects on the metal of the gun, and so it has been placed under cover in these vaults.

18 HAWK HILL

The road which goes up past the entrance to the French Prisons and the Military Prison leads to the second highest point of the Castle Rock: the area which has come to be known as Hawk Hill. There were some minor buildings in this area from perhaps as early as the late Middle Ages, but the first structures about which we know anything with tolerable certainly dated from the reign of Charles II, when a guardhouse and artillery battery were built here. However, these were superseded by the larger buildings which now stand to the north and west of the Hill: the Governor's House of 1742, and the new Barracks of 1796. By the time these buildings were completed Hawk Hill had probably become the most important part of the Castle, since the old Royal buildings up in the medieval heart of the Castle had all been put to lesser uses, and it was not until the 19th century restorations that their splendour began to be recreated.

Hawk Hill from below.

The New Barracks.

19 FOOG'S GATE

It has already been said that the entrance to the upper enclosure of the mediaeval castle was by way of the Lang Stairs, at the side of the Portcullis Gate. But, as the rest of the Castle Rock was levelled-off and provided with well-surfaced roads, it became possible to create an entrance to the upper enclosure where the surrounding rock reaches its highest point, to the east of Hawk Hill. Although we cannot be completely certain when this was first achieved, it had certainly been done by the reign of Charles II, when the existing wall was erected along the west edge of the upper enclosure. This wall was pierced by a series of openings for artillery, and by a single gate known – rather mysteriously – as Foog's Gate, set within a kink in the wall so that it could be covered by flanking fire from the neighbouring wall.

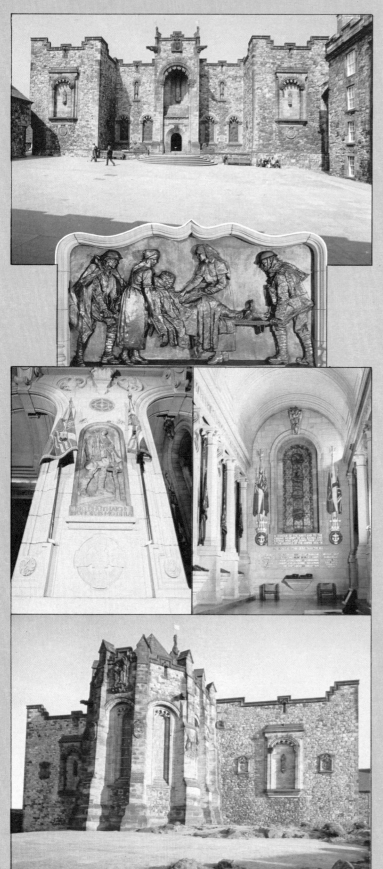

20 CROWN SQUARE

At the heart of the late mediaeval Castle is the open area now known as Crown Square, around which the parts of the Castle most closely associated with the Royal residence are ranged. However, of the four buildings which now define the Square, only two have recognisably mediaeval work in them.

21 THE SCOTTISH NATIONAL WAR MEMORIAL

The Scottish National War Memorial is the most modern of the buildings around the Square, dating in its present form from the 1920s. It occupies the site of the mediaeval church of St Mary, which had been demoted into a munition house in the 16th century. The shell of the existing building was erected in 1755 as a barracks, although it now requires a very keen eye to spot the mid-18th century work. The decision to convert it into a War Memorial was made after the Great War of 1914–18, and Sir Robert Lorimer completed his designs in 1924. It was opened by the Prince of Wales in 1927. Externally the major alterations to the existing building were the addition of a polygonal apse to the north, and the elaboration of the entrance-front towards Crown Square with sculptured decoration. Whilst the treatment of the exterior was subdued, in sympathy with the surrounding buildings, the interior was more richly treated, and is a most moving tribute to the Scottish dead. The 18th century building was transformed into a colonnaded and vaulted cross-hall, with its climax in the apse opposite the entrance, in which prominence is given to the casket containing the names of the dead. The qualities of the interior are greatly enhanced by stained glass in the windows, which is the work of Douglas Strachan.

Top to bottom
Memorial Front.
Nurses' Memorial.
Scottish Battalions'
Memorial.
Hall of Honour looking east.
Memorial Apse.

Opposite St Michael.
Casket.

22 SCOTTISH UNITED SERVICES MUSEUM

The other relatively modern structure adjacent to Crown Square is the building which now houses the Scottish United Services Museum. It occupies part of the platform which was formed by the substructures engineered at the turn of the 15th and 16th centuries for the Great Hall; there were originally an artillery house and battery on the site. The existing building was erected soon after 1708, mainly to provide quarters for officers of the garrison. It consists of two parallel ranges to either side of an enclosed corridor-like courtyard.

Private, Grenadier Company 25th Foot, now Kings Own Scottish Borderers 1751.

Top to bottom

Officers pouch. Forfar and Kincardine Artillery Volunteers, late 19th century.

Pipers of the Scots Guards about 1900.

Sergeant Ewart, Royal Scots Greys taking the Eagle of the French 45th at Waterloo 1816. Watercolour by William Wollen.

Opposite Views of the Great Hall.

26

23 THE GREAT HALL

In the earlier middle ages the hall was the main communal living space of a palace or castle, and was used to a greater or lesser extent by all members of the household. There was probably a hall on the rock at Edinburgh as early as about 600, when the warriors of the British King Mynyddog gathered in it, but that Hall – which was possibly built of timber – has vanished without trace. There are repeated references to later halls in the Castle throughout the middle ages, as for example when a new roof was provided for the Hall at the command of Robert II in the later 14th century. These too have left no surviving remains, and it is only the last of this series of buildings, the Hall built for James IV, that we really know about.

By the time that James IV started his building the function of a hall had changed considerably: although it would still have had a limited communal use, its chief purpose was now to provide a setting for great ceremonial occasions. The confined space available for such a building on the highest point of the rock summit meant that, before the Hall could be started, a level had to be obtained by constructing a massive vaulted substructure, no mean feat of engineering for the time (the vaults are now known as the French Prisons). The Hall itself was rectangular, and was lit by large windows on its south side. It was entered through a door towards its west end, separated from the main body of the Hall by timber screens to prevent draughts; the most important part of the Hall was at the east end, where the King and principal members of his court took their place. The finest single feature of the Hall was its elaborate open-timber roof, with a finely detailed supporting framework cantilevered out from the wallhead on hammer-beams; this, fortunately, is one of the few parts of the original design to be preserved intact.

The Hall has had a chequered history since it was first built. It started to be used as a barrack in 1650 and was progressively subdivided by inserted floors and walls for that purpose; it was also later used as a hospital. The decision to restore it to its original layout was made in the 19th century, and it was restored between 1887 and 1891 to the designs of Hippolyte Blanc, and at the cost of William Nelson the publisher. The end-result of the restoration is perhaps closer to a Hollywood idea of what a great hall should be than might be wished, although we should be grateful for Mr Nelson's munificence, which made it possible to reverse the earlier disfiguration.

The private accommodation for the King and his immediate household seems to have been placed at the south-east point of the rock since at least the 14th century. It was at this corner of the Castle that David II started to build a tower-house for himself in 1368, and the tower was progressively augmented and extended throughout the later Middle Ages. The nucleus of the existing Palace-building, on the east side of Crown Square, may have been first formed by a great chamber which James I is known to have built for himself at the side of the tower in the 1430s. But it was probably in the early 16th century that James IV first began to give the Palace the basis of its present form, at the same time that he was building the adjoining Great Hall. It was modified for Mary Queen of Scots and her consort, Henry Lord Darnley, and above one of the doors there is the date 1566, with the initials MAH (for *Mary and Henry*). Fifty years later it was again remodelled in anticipation of James VI's homecoming, and at that time the northern part of the range was heightened and given a more regular pattern of windows conforming to the newly classical taste of the time. The last major change to the exterior of the Palace took place in the early 19th century when the domed roof of the stair turret towards Crown Square was removed, and the turret rather absurdly heightened to take the castle's main flag-staff.

Parts of the Palace are now used by the Scottish United Services Museum, but there are two rooms which are of particular interest for the history of the Castle. One of these is a small ground-floor chamber, leading off what used to be the Queen's bed-chamber, in which Mary Queen of Scots gave birth to the future James VI; it was redecorated at the time of James VI's homecoming to commemorate the event, which was doubtless of much interest to James himself. The second room is a vaulted chamber at first-floor level, in which the Scottish Regalia of Crown, Sword and Sceptre were stored, and in which they were walled-up after the Act of Union of 1707. The vault was eventually re-opened, and the Regalia placed on display in 1818.

The Scottish Crown.

The Palace Block from below the Castle.

Painted details from the Queen's bed-chamber.

Dated stone with the initials of Mary Queen of Scots and Lord Darnley.

Mary Queen of Scots. Detail from a painting by an unknown artist.

James VI by Vanson.

25 THE HALF MOON BATTERY

It has already been mentioned that the tower house built by David II at the southeast corner of the Castle was knocked down in the course of the siege in 1573, and that the walls of the Half Moon Battery were afterwards wrapped around its ruins. From inside the present entrance to the castle it can be seen how the walls of the Battery soar above the approaches, but it is only from the level of its gun platform that it can be realised what a splendid command it gave the defenders of the Castle over the land to the east. Nevertheless, despite the advantages it gave to its defenders, it did not prevent the Castle from being taken in the two sieges of 1650 and 1689, and in the course of those two sieges the protective parapet which surmounts it was damaged to an extent that necessitated major rebuilding. The platform on top of the battery is at a similar level to the principal buildings on top of the Castle Rock, and it requires an effort of imagination to appreciate that,

because of the formation of the rock at this point, there are two stories of David's Tower still surviving beneath the platform. The existing ground-level of the Battery is carried on a series of vaults, and it is worth noting that these vaults were for a long time used as a water cistern to contain the Castle's water supply.

26 THE FOREWALL BATTERY

The history of this battery as it now stands is very similar to that of the Half Moon Battery, having been built after the siege of 1573, and repaired after the sieges of 1650 and 1689. But the earlier history of the Castle's defences at this point is rather more complicated, since the principal wall across the east end of the rock has always followed a similar line to that of the existing wall of the battery. Looking down from the wallhead it is easy to appreciate why this should have been so. On this line the Castle Rock rises sharply, leaving a narrow approach path up to a natural entrance point where the Portcullis Gate now stands; as a result defenders at wallhead level had a great advantage over unwanted visitors who were approaching the gate too closely, since the latter were in the direct field of fire from both the wall and the gate over a considerable length of their approach.

27 SAINT MARGARET'S CHAPEL

The last of the buildings to be seen within the Castle is the earliest of its surviving structures, the small chapel dedicated to St Margaret, wife of King Malcolm III, and mother of Kings Edgar, Alexander I and David I. No records survive of when this chapel was built, but on the evidence of its architecture it is likely to date from the reign of David I, who came to the throne in 1124. It is now a free-standing structure, but for many years it was linked up with other buildings and put to secular use; its intended purpose was only rediscovered in 1845, after which it was restored to what was thought to be its original form. Although externally it is an unpretentious rectangular block, internally it is rather more complex, and is divided into two parts by a fine arch decorated with zigzag ornament. At the east end, through the arch, is a semi-circular vaulted apse to contain the altar, whilst the main body of the chapel is the rectangular nave, for the congregation. The nave is also vaulted, although the present vault was constructed when the building was in use as a Powder Magazine.

Earlier vaults encapsulated in the Half Moon and Forewall Batteries.

The Forewall and Half Moon Batteries.

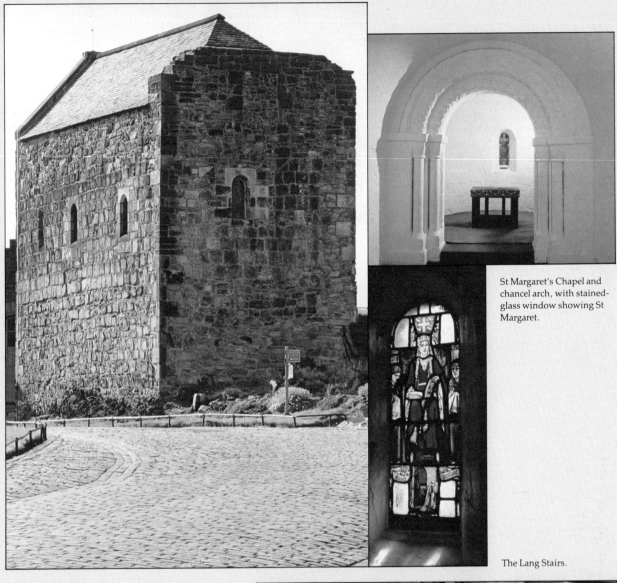

St Margaret's Chapel and chancel arch, with stained-glass window showing St Margaret.

The Lang Stairs.

28 LANG STAIRS

The visitor's route from the upper enclosure of the Castle leads down the steep winding flight of steps known as the Lang Stairs, which perpetuates the flight which was the principal approach to this most important part of the Castle throughout the Middle Ages. The staircase passes the upper storeys of the Portcullis Gate, which was rebuilt in 1886 to look like the architect's idea of what a mediaeval castle gate should be: unfortunately he failed to allow for the fact that the present gate had been built in the 1570s, by which time defenders would have been using artillery rather than bows and arrows. The gate is sometimes known as the Argyle Tower, because the 9th Earl of Argyle is thought to have spent his last days before his execution in an upper chamber of the gate.

THE EDINBURGH TATTOO

For many visitors the Castle is never more alive than when the Edinburgh Tattoo is taking place on the Esplanade, and it is not always realised that this great spectacle is a relatively recent innovation. The first Tattoo, which was staged to coincide with the first Edinburgh International Festival, took place in 1947 and was conceived on a rather modest scale. Since then the scope of the conception has enormously increased, and now an elaborate scaffold which overhangs the Esplanade on each side is necessary to accommodate the audiences which flock to see the event each year.

Printed in Scotland for Her Majesty's Stationery Office by Pillans and Wilson Ltd   Dd 630372   K2560   8/80   4005